How to Think Like a Millionaire in 30 Days
Why Changing Your Thoughts Daily is Essential to Achieving The Success You Desire

By Jean Kuhn
© 2013 Jean Kuhn

All rights reserved for
How to Think Like a Millionaire in 30 Days
Why Changing Your Thoughts Daily is Essential to Achieving The Success You Desire

No part of this workbook may be reproduced or transmitted in any form or by any means without written permission from the author.

The Strangest Secret
By Earl Nightingale
Written in 1956

Jean Kuhn

Business Coach, Speaker and Author

Jean@JeanKuhn.com

How to Think Like a Millionaire in 30 Days
Why Changing Your Thoughts Daily is Essential to Achieving The Success You Desire

By

Jean Kuhn

How To Use This Workbook

1. Make sure you read The Strangest Secret, by Earl Nightingale. I have included a copy of it at the end of this workbook. I purposefully left room for you, on the right side of each page, to make notes as ideas come to you while you read the book.

2. I am going to recommend either downloading a free 37 minute audio copy of The Strangest Secret book from the internet, or spend $3 and download it from iTunes. Here is the iTunes link: https://itunes.apple.com/us/artist/earl-nightingale/id259076118?ign-mpt=uo%3D4 You will use the recording daily during this **How to Think Like a Millionaire in 30 Days** Program. While it is great to have the book, and I have included it for you, repetitive listening is an integral part of this program. Change your habits, change your mind.

3. The value of repetitive listening is it helps us form new habits. Without repetitive listening you will actually miss the lessons from the CD. Our minds will wander while we are listening. That's why we can listen to a CD 15 times straight and on the 16th time of listening, we hear something new. There is much wisdom in this CD, and repetitive listening is the ONLY way to learn it.

4. You will find a writing assignment each day for 30 days. ***Do not*** do more than one writing assignment a day. This is a journey not a race. Think carefully about what you write. This is your personal manifesto for your goal. The value of the writing will become apparent after about day 10 when you start actually seeing some results of your actions. However, your results are completely determined by how well you follow the directions. If you think you can skip the listening or the writing, and still have the same outcome, you cannot.

   Reading the day's assignment and answering it out loud or mentally, **will not** give you the same results and more likely it will give you zero results. Don't start this program until you are ready to follow the directions. Otherwise, you will become discouraged, and you will waste your time.

5. On page 7 you will write your "clearly defined goal." Write this goal as if you have already achieved it. Think of this quote from the book, "Your mind is like good fertile soil. Your mind doesn't care what you plant it will return to you what you plant." Plant the thoughts of success by writing your goal as if you have already achieved it.

   Choose ONE goal to work on for 30 days. Don't try to accomplish 2 or 3 big goals for your first 30-Day Program. In her book, The Barefoot Executive, Carrie Wilkerson said, "It's impossible to chase two rabbits at the same time and catch either one." Earl Nightingale tells us what William James said… "only you must, then really wish these things, and wish them exclusively, and not wish at the same time a hundred other incompatible things just as strongly." Don't worry you will have plenty of time to work on other goals. William James lived in the 1800s. While he says you must "wish" these things, let me be clear, you are not "wishing" anything. You are creating a plan to follow to achieve your goal.

Be specific when writing your goal. I suggest you start your goal card with: I'm so happy and grateful that I have attracted_____ into my life. Write your clearly defined goal on a sheet of paper, until you have it worded exactly like you want it. Then write in your workbook.

Don't forget to write the quote from the Sermon on the Mount on the back of your goal card.

"Ask, And It Shall Be Given You"
"Seek, And Ye Shall Find"
"Knock, And It Shall Be Opened Unto You"

Why do you have to write that on the back, because Earl Nightingale told us to? Learn this quote, and think of it often.

Make 3 or 4 Goal note cards that say exactly the same thing. Put one by your bedside, one in your wallet or purse, one on your bathroom mirror, and another in your car. Read the card out loud every day, countless times. You don't have to do this in front of anyone, it's your brain we are working on changing.

6. The magic happens in your writing. If you don't like to write, well, you have two choices. You can stay exactly where you are, or you can do something different for 30 days that will have profound changes on your life or business. The choice is really yours. The more you write the better. You really can't write too much, however, you absolutely can write too little. You will see that you have ample room to write in your workbook. If you are using half the space or less you are not writing enough. If you are on a roll, keep writing get another sheet of paper out.

7. Be prepared. Once you set your clearly defined goal, and you have made the commitment to work on it for 30 days, people, resources and opportunities will start showing up to help you accomplish your goal. It's weird, but fun too, when you start seeing it. You have to keep your mind open, or you might miss them. Especially opportunities. Make up your mind to start saying YES when you might want to say NO. If you say no to the people, resources, and opportunities, that present themselves, you will not be able to hit your goal. Be mindful of everybody and everything in the next 30 days.

8. Make sure you are writing all of the details for each question. As you are working on this workbook, you are actually creating your "playbook" for your goal, and the one after that, and the one after that. The money is in the details.

9. Some days have multiple questions. Answer all of them. You will find questions that you don't want to answer or don't know how to answer. Answer them anyway. Give these questions more thought before you answer them. DO NOT SKIP them. These hard-to-answer questions are break-through questions. This is where you are "stuck", and you can't get "unstuck" without the answers.

10. Are you guaranteed to accomplish your goal in the next 30 days? This is a good question. It depends on a couple of things.

    1. Are you following these rules
    2. Are you listening to the audio everyday
    3. Are you doing the homework everyday
    4. Are you seeing progress as you answer the questions
    5. Once you've written the homework are you following your plan
    6. Are you taking the steps needed
    7. Are you keeping your eyes and mind open to people and opportunities

    My most successful client that participated in this course took advantage of my **How to Think Like a Millionaire in 30 Days** accountability program. She stepped way outside her comfort zone, and completely changed her thinking for 30 straight days. Her goal was to attract an additional $6000 in 30 days. She had worked hard on the daily questions, watched for people and opportunities that started showing up, and on day 29 she had attracted an additional **$60,000**. The first thing she did was to check her goal card to see if she had added an extra zero. She had not. Then she called me because she realized what had just happened. I'm not going to lie. I was pretty amazed too. Surprised? No. Amazed? Yes!

11. If you are ready to get what you really want, turn the page and get started.

Write _**all**_ of the goals, income producing ideas, challenges, all of the things you know you want to accomplish. One of these will stand out as the goal you want to achieve first and foremost above all others. Everything written here won't be worked on immediately. This is just a list of things you want to accomplish eventually.

_____

_____

_____

_____

_____

_____

_____

_____

_____

_____

_____

_____

_____

_____

_____

_____

_____

Now pick **THE** one most important item to you from the above list, and clearly define it below. Answer all 10 questions below. You will finish this section by putting it all together. Write in full complete positive sentences. Don't forget to write as if you have already achieved your goal. Of course you feel silly doing this. We all do. I use to. Remember, you are the only one seeing this playbook

1. What does success look like to you?
2. What does it feel like?
3. What are you going to do when you reach the goal?
4. Who are the people you will you need to achieve this goal?
5. What resources or tools will you need to achieve this goal?
6. How will achieving this goal, change your life?
7. Write down the steps you believe you will need to start taking.
8. If the goal is more money how much do you want and what will you do with it?
9. What steps do you need to take to achieve this goal?
10. If you don't know, how can you find out?

The most important thing for me to accomplish in the next 30 days is:

_____

_____

_____

_____

_____

_____

_____

_____

_____

_____

Now it's time to write your goal card. Remember you are writing it as if you have already achieved it. I recommend starting with: I am so happy and grateful that I have attracted……….. Tomorrow you start Day 1.

Day 1

Listen to the audio recording of The Strangest Secret

Earl Nightingale defines success: "Success is the progressive realization of a worthy ideal." What is your worthy ideal? This is different from your goal card, because today you are taking action toward your goal.

How do you define success with your goal for this 30-Day Test? Define one or two actions steps you will take today to work toward that goal.

_____

_____

_____

_____

_____

_____

_____

_____

_____

_____

Day 2

Listen to the audio recording of The Strangest Secret

Earl Nightingale said, "Men simply don't think." What do you think he meant by that? What are you thinking regarding your goal today?

Day 3

Listen to the audio recording of The Strangest Secret

"Above all ... don't worry! Worry brings fear, and fear is crippling. The only thing that can cause you to worry during your test is trying to do it all yourself. Know that all you have to do is hold your goal before you; everything else will take care of itself."

"Remember also to keep calm and cheerful, don't let petty things annoy you and get you off course."

If, You Become What You Think About, and you spend your time worrying about IF and HOW you are going to hit your goal, do you see how you are self-sabotaging? That means you are thinking more about NOT hitting your goal than you are thinking about hitting your goal….and, we become what we think about, therefore, you can't possibly hit your goal if you are worried about not hitting it. Whew!

Make a list of 5 reasons you have no reason to worry. Even if you don't believe your reasons right this minute, make a list anyway and write it in such a way that you don't need to worry because you have already hit your goal.

_____

_____

_____

_____

_____

_____

_____

_____

_____

_____

Day 4

Listen to the audio recording of The Strangest Secret – Remember the key to change in material like this is repetitive listening.

"Rollo May, the distinguished psychiatrist, wrote in his wonderful book called: *Man's Search for Himself,* "**The opposite of courage in our society is not cowardice - it is conformity."** 95% of people conform. They work because that is what they are supposed to do. Those that conform believe that life is shaped by circumstances, things that happen to them.

How are you choosing to be different today in your thoughts and your actions? How are you stepping outside of your comfort zone today? What courageous steps will you take today toward your goal? Remember the magic is in the details.

Day 5

Listen to the audio recording of The Strangest Secret.

True growth, both personally and professionally, happens when you are uncomfortable. You become uncomfortable when that little voice in your head starts trash talking you. It will tell you that you aren't smart enough, you're too fat, you aren't pretty enough, others will laugh at you, no one else has ever done that why do you think you can, you are too old to go back to school or a thousand other negative things. When you do something that little voice doesn't agree with you start to feel uncomfortable. Right there, that uncomfortable feeling…..that is where your growth happens.

It won't just be that little voice in your head; it will also be your friends and family. When this happens you have to find the courage to remove yourself from the negative talk, give yourself a pep talk, and keep pushing forward. This is the only way you are going to succeed. I have written a couple of blogs about this too. Feel free to check them out at these links: A Powerful Business Lesson From Oprah's Last Show and My Self-Talk Was Mean To Me. You can find these on my website: http://JeanKuhn.com/blog.

Today, what is your self-talk saying to you? How are you answering it? And, what are you learning about yourself?

_____

_____

_____

_____

_____

_____

_____

_____

_____

Day 6

Listen to the audio recording of The Strangest Secret.

"A success is anyone who is pursuing deliberately a predetermined goal, because that's what he or she decided to do ... deliberately. But only one out of 20 does that. That is why today there is really not any competition unless we make it for ourselves. Instead of competing, all we have to do is create."

"People with goals succeed because they know where they are going." Where you "going" TODAY and what are you doing to get there?

List 5 Action Steps you can take today to move you closer to your goal.

_____

_____

_____

_____

_____

_____

_____

_____

_____

_____

_____

_____

_____

Take ACTION on these steps – NOW!!! TODAY!!! Don't let anyone or anything stop you from completing these items. You are **UNSTOPPABLE!!!**

Day 7

Listen to the audio recording of The Strangest Secret

We Become What We Think About.

What are you thinking about today? Are you thinking: I don't have enough: Enough time, enough money, enough employees or enough good help, too many bills on my desk, too much to read, I need a vacation, but can't afford one? If any of this sounds like you, you need to stop. Listen to the recording again right now.

When you are thinking about all that you don't have, you are blocking your blessings. All you are going to get is more of what you are thinking about. Not enough. Today make a list of all of the things you are grateful for. Meaning, make a list of all of the things you do have, not what you don't have. Take a moment as you make the list to just say, Thank you to your higher power for all you do have. When we can be grateful for everything that we have, we attract more good things.

When you think about, "**We Become What We Think About**" are you thinking about your goal card and the goal you have set for yourself. You should be thinking of your goal in a pleasant way every single day.

Make a list of 10 things you are grateful for today. Next, write why you are grateful you have accomplished your goal. (Remember, we believe that we have already achieved it.) Finally today, write 3 action items you can accomplish today toward your goal.

_____

_____   _____

_____

_____

_____

_____

_____

_____

_____

Day 8

Listen to the audio recording of the Strangest Secret.

"Our doubts are traitors, and make us lose the good we oft might win by fearing to attempt."

What doubts are you dealing with right now? Are you fearful this program will not work? Are you doubtful the action steps you have been taking are not paying off? Have you actually completed your action steps or were you fearful of even attempting them? You are not alone. All of us struggle with fear. I have written a couple blogs on fear that you can find on my website http://JeanKuhn.com. Here is a good one: You Have Spoiled Me From Working For Anyone Else.

Today, write down any doubts you are having. No details about them. Now get a marker, preferable red, and draw a big fat line through them. Below your doubts write yourself a reminder about how awesome it feels to have achieved your 30 Day goal. Remind yourself about what it means to have accomplished it. Remind yourself that if you can accomplish this one goal, you can accomplish anything "you set your mind to." Picture the smile on your face when you tell those who said you never would finish, that not only did you finish, you exceeded your expectations.

Doubts:_____

_____

_____

_____   _____

You didn't think I was going to give you a lot of space for writing negative thoughts did you. Now draw that line through them.

Reminder:_____

_____

_____

_____

_____

That was Easy!

Day 9

Listen to the audio recording of The Strangest Secret

Failure Leads to Success. Yes Really! Take a look at this written by Benny Hsu.

People who found success despite failures

<u>Colonel Sanders</u> : The founder of KFC. He started his dream at 65 years old! He got a social security check for only $105 and was mad. Instead of complaining he did something about it.

He thought restaurant owners would love his fried chicken recipe, use it, sales would increase, and he'd get a percentage of it. He drove around the country knocking on doors, sleeping in his car, wearing his white suit.

Do you know how many times people said no till he got one yes? **1009 times!**

<u>Walt Disney</u>: The man who gave us Disney World and Mickey Mouse. His first animation company went bankrupt. He was fired by a news editor because he lacked imagination. Legend has it he was **turned down 302 times** before he got financing for creating Disney World.

<u>Albert Einstein</u>: He didn't speak till he was four and didn't read till seven. His parents and teachers thought he was mentally handicapped. He only turned out to win a Nobel prize and be the face of modern physics.

<u>Richard Branson</u>: He's a billionaire mogul of Virgin but has had his share of failures. Remember Virgin Cola or Virgin credit cards? Probably not. He's lost hundreds of millions of dollars but has not let failure stop him. When you're rich like him you can rent his private island for <u>$53,000 a night</u>.

<u>Mark Cuban</u>: The billionaire owner of the NBA's Dallas Mavericks got rich when he sold his company to Yahoo for $5.9 billion in stock. He admitted he was terrible at his early jobs. His parents wanted him to have a normal job. So he tried carpentry but hated it. He was a short order cook but a terrible one. He waited tables but couldn't open a bottle of wine. He says of <u>his failures,</u>

"I've learned that it doesn't matter how many times you failed," Cuban says. "You only have to be right once. I tried to sell powdered milk. I was an idiot lots of times, and I learned from them all."

Vincent Van Gogh: He only **sold one painting** in his lifetime! Just one to a friend. Despite that he kept painting and finished over 800 pieces. Now everyone wants to buy them and his most expensive painting is valued at $142.7 million.

Theodor Seuss Giesel: Dr. Seuss gave us *Cat in the Hat* and *Green Eggs and Ham*. Books every child reads. At first many didn't think he would succeed. **27 different publishers rejected** Dr. Seuss's first book *To Think That I Saw It on Mulberry Street.*

John Grisham: The American author first was a lawyer who loved to write. His first book *A Time to Kill* took three years to write. The book was **rejected 28 times** until he got one yes for a 5,000 copy print. He's sold over 250 million total copies of his books.

Steven Spielberg: He applied and was **denied two times** to the prestigious University of Southern California film school. Instead he went to Cal State University in Long Beach.

He went on to direct some of the biggest movie blockbusters in history. Now he's worth $2.7 billion and in **1994 got an honorary degree** from the film school that rejected him twice.

Stephen King: His first book *Carrie* was **rejected 30 times** and he threw it in the trash. His wife retrieved it out of the trash and encouraged him to resubmit it. The rest is history. He has sold more than 350 million copies of his books. (He's also made many adults fear clowns too.)

Stephenie Meyer: The author of the crazy *Twilight* series said the inspiration from the book came from a dream. She finished it in three months but never intended to publish it until a friend suggested she should.

She wrote 15 letters to literary agencies. Five didn't reply. Nine rejected. One gave her a chance. Then eight publishers auctioned for the right to publish *Twilight*. She got a three book deal worth $750,000. In 2010, Forbes reported she earned $40 million.

Tim Ferris: The man behind the *4 Hour Workweek,* who changed how many people's view work and life, was **rejected by 26 publishers** before one gave him a chance. It's been on the bestseller's list for years, sold all over the world, and last year published *The 4 Hour Body* that went to #1 on the New York Times bestsellers list.

The Beatles: They were rejected by many record labels. In a famous rejection, the label said, ""guitar groups are on the way out" and "the Beatles have no future in show business".

After that the Beatles signed with EMI, brought Beatlemania to the United States, and became the greatest band in history.

Michael Jordan: He's famous for being cut from his high school basketball team. He turned out to be the greatest basketball player but never let failure deter him. I love this quote…

"I have missed more than 9,000 shots in my career. I have lost almost 300 games. On 26 occasions I have been entrusted to take the game winning shot, and I missed. I have failed over and over and over again in my life. And that is why I succeed."

Thomas Edison: No list of success from failures would be complete without the man who gave us many inventions including the light bulb. He knew failure wouldn't stop him.

If I find 10,000 ways something won't work, I haven't failed. I am not discouraged, because every wrong attempt discarded is another step forward.

There is no success without failure

So now, how does your failures look in comparison? What have you failed at this week, and how did you handle it?

_____

_____

_____

_____

_____

_____

_____

_____

_____

Day 10

Listen to the audio recording of The Strangest Secret.

My favorite quote from the The Strangest Secret is, "George Bernard Shaw said, 'People are always blaming their circumstances for what they are. I don't believe in circumstances. The people who get on in this world are the people who get up and look for the circumstances they want, and if they can't find them, make them.'" What have you "made" happen in the first 9 days? What is your measurable progress?

Day 11

Listen to the audio recording of The Strangest Secret.

Are you reading your goal card in the morning, during the day, and at night? The person who has no goal doesn't know where he or she is going. Make a list of 6 action items you are committed to achieving to help you hit your goal, and what steps will you take for each item **today?**

Day 12

Listen to the audio recording of The Strangest Secret – Remember the key to change in material like this is repetitive listening.

"Now how does it work? Why do we become what we think about?"

"Well I'll tell you how it works as far as we know. To do this I want to talk about a situation that parallels the human mind."

"The human mind is much like a farmer's land. Suppose a farmer has some land. And it is good fertile land. The land gives the farmer a choice. He may plant in that land whatever he chooses."

"The land doesn't care what is planted. It's up to the farmer to make the decision.
Remember we are comparing the human mind to the farmers land because, the mind, like the land, doesn't care what you plant in it. It will return what you plant, but it doesn't care what you plant."

"Let's say that the farmer has two seeds in his hand - one a seed of corn, the other is nightshade, a deadly poison. He digs two little holes in the earth and he plants seeds, one corn, the other nightshade."

"He covers up the holes, waters, and takes care of the land. What will happen?"

"Invariably, the land will return what is planted.
As it is written in the Bible "As ye sow, so shall ye reap.""

"Remember, the land doesn't care. It will return poison in just as wonderful abundance as it will corn. So up come the two plants - one corn, one poison."

"The human mind is far more fertile, far more incredible and mysterious than the land, but it works the same way. It does not care what we plant ... success ... or failure. A concrete, worth-while goal ... or confusion, misunderstanding, fear, anxiety, and so on. But what we plant it must return to us."

"The human mind is the last great unexplored continent on earth. It contains riches beyond our wildest dreams. It will return anything we want to plant."

What are you planting in your mind today? What ideas are starting to come to you as you listen to the audio recording over and over? One of the ideas that came to me was this workbook. Are your writing the ideas down that come to you? Don't take action on the new ideas just yet. Wait till your 30 Day Program is over, then start your next project. Write here what you are thinking about today, and any new ideas you are having that you want to work on.

Day 13

Listen to the audio recording of The Strangest Secret.

"The human mind is not used because we take it for granted. Familiarity breeds contempt. It can do any kind of job we assign to it, but generally speaking, we use it for little jobs instead of big important ones. Universities have proved that most of us are operating on about ten percent or less of our abilities."

Assuming this is correct, which I believe it is, what would you accomplish with the 90% of your brain power you aren't using? Think outside the box today of 3 action items you could use to help you accomplish your goal if you were using the other 90% of your brain power. Feel free to ask others for help on this one. Make sure you ask someone who is using at least 20% of their brain power. Write down your 3 action items, and action steps you can take to accomplish these items. **Then Do It!!!**

Day 14

Listen to the audio recording of The Strangest Secret

"First, it is understanding emotionally as well as intellectually, that we literally become what we think about, that we must control our thoughts if we are to control our lives. It is understanding fully that "As ye sow, so shall ye reap."

'Second, it is cutting away all fetters from the mind and permitting it to soar as it was divinely designed to do. It is the realization that your limitations are self-imposed, and the opportunities for you today are enormous beyond belief. It is rising above narrow-minded pettiness and prejudice.'

'And third, it is using all your courage to force yourself to think positively on your own problems. To set a definite and clearly defined goal for yourself and to let your marvelous mind think about your goal from all possible angles; to let your imagination speculate freely upon many different possible solutions; to refuse to believe that there are any circumstances sufficiently strong to defeat you in the accomplishment of your purpose."

"We must control our thinking." This is probably the most difficult part of Earl Nightingale's 30-Day Test. Why is this difficult? Because we choose our thoughts 100% of the time. Whatever you are thinking about, you are choosing those thoughts. When the negative thoughts or negative self-talk starts invading your head, you **have to choose** **to make a conscious effort to change your thoughts**. If you keep doing this over and over, eventually your brain just starts thinking differently. It starts looking to the positive instead of the negative, and this is exactly why you have to do this exercise for the full 30 days. Keep going you're doing great!

Today, what thoughts are you choosing to think, and how are you doing that?

_____

_____

_____

_____

_____

_____

Day 15

Listen to the audio recording of the Strangest Secret.

If you have been faithfully following this 30-Challenge Program, then you have earned a reward today. Listen to the recording, and take the rest of the day off. Continue to think about your goal. If you have not faithfully been following the program, make a list of three action items you intend to accomplish today. For each of the three action items, add three action steps you can take today to more your goal forward.

If you are an over-achiever feel free to keep on working, you'll be glad you did.

Day 16

Listen to the audio recording of The Strangest Secret.

"Sometimes the return will not come from those you serve, but it must come to you from someplace, because that is the law. For every action, there is an equal and opposite reaction."

As you keep working toward your goal, keep the above thought in mind. "Sometimes the return will not come from those you serve, but it must come to you from someplace, because that is the law." Are you mindful of the people and the opportunities that have started showing up in your life to help you achieve your goal? What people and what opportunities have shown up in your life.

What this means is, let's say you set your goal to earn more money. You may be working your business harder to achieve your goal. You think the extra money is going to come from extra sales that you have been working on. That may be true, you may earn extra money from extra sales you brought in, but you may receive a rebate on your insurance you weren't expecting. You may get an inheritance you weren't expecting. You may get an invitation to meet with someone you don't know who makes you an offer you did not see coming. These are NOT coincidences. The people and opportunities that show up are because of an energy you are emitting. Your energy and the energy of the people and or opportunities that are showing up are the same level. This is called The Law of Attraction.

Please don't misunderstand. While the Law of Attraction is at play here, and your thoughts have changed to ones of positive, deliberate thoughts, you absolutely CAN NOT think yourself successful. You have been taking action everyday working toward your goal. The thoughts AND the actions are what is attracting the people and opportunities to you.

If you were looking for extra money, you should be mindful of every extra dollar that comes your way during this 30-Day Program. Whatever your goal, you should be mindful of the people and opportunities that present themselves to you. Check out my blog post titled: Can You See An Opportunity When It Smacks You In The Face? You can find that on my website: http://JeanKuhn.com/blog

What people and opportunities have shown themselves to you since you started this program? Did you recognize them immediately? How did they help you?

_____

_____

_____

_____

Day 17

Listen to the audio recording of The Strangest Secret

"As you go daily through your 30 day test period, your success will always be measured by the quality and quantity of service you render, and money is a yardstick for measuring this service. No person can get rich themselves, unless they first enrich others. There are no exceptions to a law."

Who have you served? How have you worked to enrich others? Did you give them the best that you had in terms of quality of service and product? How might you serve more people?

Day 18

Listen to the audio recording of The Strangest Secret.

The seeds in your mind's fertile soil are sprouting and growing. What is growing? What successes have you seen so far? What progress have you made toward your goal as of today? How close to your goal are you? New ideas come from the details.

Day 19

"Dorothea Brande, the outstanding editor and writer, discovered it for herself and talks about it in her fine book "Wake up and Live". Her entire philosophy is reduced to the words: **"Act as though it were impossible to fail."** She made her own test, with sincerity and faith, and her entire life was changed to overwhelming success."

What would you do to achieve your goal if you knew it was impossible to fail? Write down all of the ideas and steps you would take if you knew you could NOT fail.

___

___

___

___

___

___

___

___

___

___

___

___

___

___

___

___

___

Now do them!

Day 20

Listen to the audio recording of The Strangest Secret.

Are you starting to notice the people without goals? If not, get out and meet people, and if yes, what are you seeing possibly for the first time? How do you differ from those with no real goals?

Day 21

Listen to the audio recording of The Strangest Secret.

Earl Nightingale tells us, "In your spare time during your test period read books that will help you. Read at least 15 minutes each day. Inspirational books like The Bible, Dorothea Brande's "Wake up and Live" if you can still find a copy, "The Magic of Believing" by Claude Bristol, "Think and Grow Rich" by Napoleon Hill, and **other books** that instruct and inspire."

Nothing great was every accomplished without inspiration. Have you read any of the above mentioned books?

Mr. Nightingale wrote his list of reading material in 1956, I have put together a list of some of my favorite books that you might enjoy. You can find my list at:

http://JeanKuhn.com/resources

What non-fiction are you reading now that is motivational and/or inspirational? What is next on the list and why?

_____
_____
_____
_____
_____
_____
_____
_____
_____
_____
_____

Day 22

Listen to the audio recording of The Strangest Secret

"Each day for this 30 day test, do more than you have to do."

"In addition to maintaining a cheerful positive outlook, give of yourself more than you have ever done before. Do this knowing that your returns in life must be in direct proportion to what you give."

"The moment you decide on a goal to work toward, you immediately are a successful person. You are then in that rare and successful category of people who know where they are going. Out of every 100 people, you belong to the top five."

How have you done more than necessary in the past 20 days? After you answer this question write 3 action items you can commit to doing today to help you achieve your goal. Now write 3 action steps for each action item, and complete these 9 tasks today.

Day 23

Listen to the audio recording of The Strangest Secret

With one week left to go, what is the best thing you have learned about yourself? What has been the best accomplishment you have made toward your goal? Which action item has taken you the furthest toward meeting your goal? The details are crucially important here. Make sure you include all of them.

Day 24

Listen to the audio recording of The Strangest Secret.

By now, you should be displaying a new "attitude". Has anyone noticed your different attitude? If so, what have they said? If not, maybe you are not displaying a calm, peaceful, grateful, cheerful attitude. If not, write a list of ways you can not only change your attitude, but a way you can show it to others.

_____

_____

_____

_____

_____

_____

_____

_____

_____

_____

_____

_____

_____

_____

_____

_____

Day 25

Listen to the audio recording of The Strangest Secret

If you are finding yourself bored with the CD, there is a problem. If you are finding yourself sometimes "zoning" out, that is OK? Keep listening. The message is slowly working its way into your subconscious where you want it to live.

Now, if you are nauseated by listening to it, my guess is that a couple things are going on here. 1) you don't really want to change. You are not looking for the value of this material. That is OK, you don't have to change. You can most certainly keep doing what you have been doing. 2) You don't really believe this material works. That is OK too. Not everyone is supposed to be successful. Only the people who realize that their thoughts really can become things are destined for success.

Or, you might not be ready now, but don't give up on this material. Give it another try. It's only 30 days, you have nothing to lose and a life to win according to Earl Nightingale.

What would you do differently the next time you do the **How to Think Like a Millionaire in 30 Days program.**

_____

_____

_____

_____

_____

_____

_____

_____

_____

Day 26

Listen to audio recording of The Strangest Secret

Are you beginning to understand that your limitations are self-imposed, and your opportunities are enormous? Don't give up now, this is really only the beginning of what you will be able to achieve. Name 3 self-imposed limitations that you either have or had when you started this course. Describe how you were able to free yourself from each one. What was your "Aha moment" when you realized you had self-imposed limitations.

_____

_____

_____

_____

_____

_____

_____

_____

_____

_____

_____

_____

_____

_____

_____

Day 27

Listen to the audio recording of The Strangest Secret.

"Stop thinking of all of the reasons why you cannot be successful, and instead, think of all the reasons why you can."

"Change the image you have of yourself by writing out a description of the person you would like to be."

"Act the part of the successful person you have decided to become."

All 3 quotes above are from Earl Nightingale's The Strangest Secret. Please write a reply to each of the above statements below.

_____

_____

_____

_____

_____

_____

_____

_____

_____

_____

_____

_____

_____

Day 28

Listen to the audio recording of The Strangest Secret.

You are almost there!!! Don't quit right before the finish line. Two more days! Today how are you "pushing through" to the end? Make a list of 5 steps you will take today to keep moving forward.

Day 29

Listen to the audio recording of The Strangest Secret

You may or may not have accomplished your clearly defined goal. If you haven't, how close are you? What will it take to finish? Obviously, not every goal is attainable in 30 short days, but no goals are attainable unless you start. If you followed this workbook, listened to the CD, and answered the questions every day, I have no doubt that you are well on your way to success. This workbook has become your "Playbook" with many, many action steps. Go back and see if you have completed every step you wrote down. If not, why? If it is still a viable idea, do it.

Today write a short paragraph about where you actually are toward reaching your goal. If you have not hit it, write what steps you need to take to finish. Then act on those steps.

Day 30

Listen to the audio recording of The Strangest Secret. Just so you can say you finished the 30 days.

Thoughts without actions are just daydreams. Today let yourself dream big. If you could be, do or have anything in life you want, what would it be? Now, if you were to do this TEST again, would this be your next goal? Why or why not? Don't forget the details.

What does your big dream look like to you? What does it feel like? What are you going to do when you reach the dream? How will you celebrate? Who do you need to help you achieve this dream? What resources or tools do you need to achieve this dream? How will achieving this dream change your life? If the dream is more money what will you do with it? What steps do you need to take to achieve this dream? If you don't know, how can you find out? If you don't know how to find out, email me, and I will tell you the answer. Jean@JeanKuhn.com

_____

_____

_____

_____

_____

_____

_____

_____

_____

_____

Congratulations for completing this course!

I hope you are proud of how hard you have worked, what you have accomplished and all you have become.

Please share your success stores with me at: Jean@JeanKuhn.com

I am always amazed by what people experience during this 30 Day Accountability Program. Never surprised, but always amazed.

The Strangest Secret

By

Earl Nightingale

I'd like to tell you about The Strangest Secret in the World.

Not long ago Albert Schweitzer the great Doctor and Nobel Prize winner was being interviewed in London and the reporter asked him, "Doctor, what is wrong with men today?" The great doctor was silent a moment, and then he said, "Men simply don't think." And it is about this that I want to talk with you.

We live today in a golden age. This is an era that man has looked forward, dreamed of, and worked toward for thousands of years. But since it is here we pretty well take it for granted. We in America are particularly fortunate to live in the richest land that ever existed on the face of the earth. A land of abundant opportunity for everyone, but do you know what happens?

Let's take 100 individuals who start even at the age of 25. Do you have any idea what will happen to those men by the time they are 65?

These 100 men, who all start even at the age of 25, believe they're going to be successful. If you ask any one of these men if he wanted to be a success he'd tell you that he did. And you'd notice that he was eager toward life, that there was a certain sparkle to his eye, an erectness to his carriage, and life seemed like a pretty interesting adventure to him.

But by the time they're 65, one will be rich,
four will be financially independent, 5 will still be working
54 will be broke. Now think a moment: Out of the 100, only five make the grade!

Why do so many fail?
What has happened to the sparkle that was there when they were 25?

What's become of the dreams, the hopes, the plans?
Why is there such a large disparity between what these men intended to do and what they actually accomplished?

When we say about 5% achieve success, we have to define success. And here's definition. **"Success is the progressive realization of a worthy ideal."**

If a man is working toward a predetermined goal and knows where he's going, that man is a success. If he's not doing that he's a failure.

"Success is the progressive realization of a worthy ideal."

Rollo May, the distinguished psychiatrist, wrote a wonderful book called: "Man's Search for Himself". And in this book he says, **"The opposite of courage in our society is not cowardice - it is conformity."**

And there you have the trouble today, its conformity. People acting like everyone else, without knowing why, without knowing where they're going.

Now think of it. In America right now there are over 14 million people 65 years of age and over, and about 13 million of these 14 million are broke. They are dependent on someone else for life's necessities.

Now we learn to read by the time we're seven. We learn to make a living by the time we're 25. Usually by that time we are not only making a living, we're supporting a family, and yet by the time we're 65, we haven't learned how to become financially independent in the richest land that has ever been known.

Why? **We conform,** and the trouble is that we're acting like the wrong percentage group - the 95% who don't succeed.

Now why do these people conform?

Well, they don't know really. These people believe that their lives are shaped by circumstances, by things that happen to them, by exterior forces. They're outer directed people.

A survey was made one time that covered a lot of men, working men, and these men were asked this question, "Why do you work?" "Why do you get up in the morning?" 19 out of 20 had no idea.

If you ask them they will say, "Everyone goes to work in the morning." And that is the reason they do it - because everyone else is doing it.

Now let's get back to our definition of success. Who succeeds?

The only man who succeeds is the man who is progressively realizing a worthy ideal. He's the man who says, "I am going to become this", and then begins to work toward that goal.

I'll tell you the successful people are. A success is the school teacher who is teaching school because that's what she wanted to do.

The success is the woman who's a wife and mother because she wanted to become a wife and mother and is doing a good job of it.

The success is the man who runs the corner gas station because that's what he wanted to do.

The success is the successful salesman who wants to become a top notch salesperson and grow and build within his organization.

A success is anyone who is doing deliberately a predetermined job, because that's what he decided to do ... deliberately.

But only one out of 20 does that.

That's why today there isn't really any competition unless we make it for ourselves. Instead of competing, all we have to do is create.

Now for twenty years I looked for the key which would determine what would happen to a human being. Was there a key, I wanted to know, which would make the future a promise that we could foretell to a large extent. Was there a key that would guarantee a person's becoming successful if he only knew about it and knew how to use it? Well there is such a key and I've found it.

Have you ever wondered why so many men work so hard and honestly without ever achieving anything in particular? And others don't seem to work hard, yet seem to get everything? They have the "magic touch." You've heard people say about someone, "Everything he touches turns to gold."

Have you ever noticed that a man who becomes successful tends to continue to become successful? And on the other hand, have you noticed how a man who is a failure tends to continue to fail?

It's because of goals. Some of us have them, some don't. People with goals succeed because they know where they are going.

Now think of a ship leaving a harbor. And think of it with the complete voyage mapped out and planned. The captain and crew know exactly where it's is going and how long it will take - it has a definite goal. Nine-thousand-nine-hundred ninety-nine times out of 10,000, it will get to where it started out to get.

Now let's take another ship, just like the first, only let's not put a crew on it, or a captain at the helm. Let's give it no aiming point, no goal, no destination. We just start the engines and let it go. I think you'll agree with me that if it gets out of the harbor at all, it will either sink or wind up on some deserted beach - a derelict. It can't go any place because it has no destination and no guidance.

It's the same with a human being.

Take the salesman for example. There is no other person in the world today with the future of a good salesman! Selling is the world's highest paid profession, if we're good at it and if we know where you are going. Every company needs top notched salesmen, and they reward those men, the sky is the limit for them. But how many can you find?

Someone once said, the human race is fixed, not to prevent the strong from winning, but to prevent the weak from losing.

The American economy today can be likened to a convoy in time of war. The entire economy is slowed down to protect its weakest link, just as the convoy had to go at the speed that will permit its slowest vessel to remain in formation.

That's why it's so easy to make a living today. It takes no particular brains or talent to make a living and support a family today. So we have a plateau of so-called "security", if that is what a person is looking for. But we do have to decide how high above this plateau we want to aim for.

Now let's get back to the Strangest Secret in The World, the story I wanted to tell you today.

Why do men with goals succeed in life, and men without them fail? Well, let me tell you something which, if you really understand it, will alter your life immediately. If you understand completely what I'm going to tell you from this moment on, your life will never be the same again.

You will suddenly find that good luck just seems to be attracted to you. The things you want just seem to fall in line. And from now on you won't have the problems, the worries, the gnawing lump of anxiety that perhaps you have experienced before. Doubt, fear well they'll be things of the past.

Here is the key to success, and, the key to failure.

"We become what we think about".

Now let me say that again.
"We become what we think about".

Throughout all history, the great wise men and teachers, philosophers, and prophets have disagreed with one another on many different things. It is only on this one point that they are in complete and unanimous agreement.

Listen to what Marcus Aurelius, the great Roman Emperor, said: He said, "A man's life is what his thoughts make of it."

Disraeli said this: "Everything comes if a man will only wait. I've brought myself after long meditation to the conviction that a human being with a settled purpose must accomplish it, and that nothing can resist a will that will stake even existence for its fulfillment."

Ralph Waldo Emerson said this, "A man is what he thinks about all day long."

William James said: "The greatest discovery of my generation is that human beings can alter their lives by altering their attitudes of mind."

And he also said, "We need only in cold blood act as if the thing in question were real, and it will become infallibly real by growing into such a connection with our life that it will become real. It will become so knit with habit and emotion that our interests in it will be those which characterize belief."

He also said this, "If you only care enough for a result, you will almost certainly obtain it." If you wish to be rich, you will be rich. If you wish to be learned, you will be learned. If you wish to be good, you will be good. Only you must, then really wish these things, and wish them exclusively, and not wish at the same time a hundred other incompatible things just as strongly."

Dr. Norman Vincent Peale said this, "This is one of the greatest laws in the universe. Fervently do I wish I had discovered it as a very young man. It dawned upon me much later in life, and I found it to be one of the greatest, if not my greatest discovery outside my relationship to God."

And the great law briefly and simply stated is: "If you think in negative terms, you will get negative results. If you think in positive terms, you will achieve positive results. That is the simple fact, which is at the basis of an astonishing law of prosperity and success. In three words: Believe and Succeed."

William Shakespeare put it this way, "Our doubts are traitors and make us lose the good we oft might win by fearing to attempt."

George Bernard Shaw said: "People are always blaming their circumstances for what they are. I don't believe in circumstances. The people who get on in this world are the people who get up and look for the circumstances they want, and if they can't find them, make them.

Well, it's pretty apparent, isn't it? And every person who discovered this, for a while, believed that he was the first to work it out.

"We become what we think about."

Now it stands to reason that a person who is thinking about a concrete and worthwhile goal is going to reach it, because that's what he's thinking about. And we become what we think about.

Conversely, the man who has no goal, who doesn't know where he's are going, and whose thoughts must therefore be thoughts of confusion, and anxiety, and fear, and worry becomes what he thinks about. Their life becomes one of frustration, fear, anxiety, and worry.

And if he thinks about nothing ... he becomes nothing.

Now how does it work? Why do we become what we think about?

Well I'll tell you how it works as far as we know. To do this I want to talk about a situation that parallels the human mind.

Suppose a farmer has some land and it is good fertile land. The land gives the farmer a choice. He may plant in that land whatever he chooses. The land doesn't care. It's up to the farmer to make the decision.

Now remember we're comparing the human mind with the land because, the mind, like the land, doesn't care what you plant in it. It will return what you plant, but it doesn't care what you plant.

Now let's say that the farmer has two seeds in his hand - one a seed of corn, the other is nightshade, a deadly poison. He digs two little holes in the earth and he plants both seeds, one corn, the other nightshade.

He covers up the holes, waters, and takes care of the land. And What will happen?

Invariably, the land will return what is planted.
As it's written in the Bible "As ye sow, so shall ye reap."

Remember, the land doesn't care. It will return poison in just as wonderful abundance as it will corn. So up come the two plants - one corn, one poison.

Now the human mind is far more fertile, far more incredible and mysterious than the land, but it works the same way. It doesn't not care what we plant ... success ... failure. A concrete, worth-while goal ... or confusion, misunderstanding, fear, anxiety, and so on. But what we plant it will return to us.

You see, the human mind is the last great unexplored continent on the earth. It contains riches beyond our wildest dreams. It will return anything we want to plant.

Now you might say, well if that is true why don't people use their minds more? Well I think they've figured out an answer to that too.

Our mind comes as standard equipment at birth. It's free, and things that are given to us for nothing, we place little value on. Things that we pay money for, we value.

The paradox is that exactly the reverse is true. Everything that's really worthwhile in life came to us free, our mind, our soul, our body, our hopes, our dreams, our ambitions, our intelligence, our love of family and children and friends. All these priceless possessions are free.

But the things that cost us money are actually very cheap and can be replaced at any time. A good man can be completely wiped out and make another fortune. He can do that several times. Even if our home burns down, we can rebuild it. But the things we got for nothing, we can never replace.

The human mind isn't used merely because we take it for granted. Familiarity breeds contempt. It can do any kind of job we assign to it, but generally speaking, we use it for little jobs instead of big important ones. Universities have proved that most of us are operating on about ten percent of our abilities.

Decide now, what is it you want? Plant your goal in your mind. It's the most important decision you'll ever make in your entire life.

Do you want to be an outstanding salesman? A better worker at your particular job? Do you want to go places in your company? ... in your community? All you've got to do is plant that seed in your mind, care for it, work steadily towards your goal, and it will become a reality.

It not only will, there's no way that it cannot. You see, that is a law - like the laws of Sir Isaac Newton, the laws of gravity. If you get on top of a building and jump off, you'll always go down - you'll never go up. And it's the same with all the other laws of nature. They always work. They're inflexible.

Think about your goal in a relaxed, positive way. Picture yourself in your mind's eye as having already achieved this goal. See yourself doing the things you will be doing when you've reached your goal.

Ours has been called a Phenobarbital Age, the age of ulcers and nervous breakdowns. At a time when medical research has raised us to a new plateau of good health and longevity, far too many of us worry ourselves into an early grave trying to cope with things in our own little personal ways, without learning a few great laws that will take care of everything for us.

These things we bring on ourselves through our habitual way of thinking. Every one of us is the sum total of his own thoughts. He is where he is, because that is exactly where he really wants to be whether he'll admit that or not.

Each of us must live off the fruit of his thoughts in the future, because what you think today and tomorrow - next month and next year - will mold your life and determine your future. You're guided by your mind.

I remember one time I was driving through Arizona. I saw one of those giant earth-moving machines roaring along the road at about 35 miles an hour with what looked like 20 tons of dirt in it - a tremendous, incredible machine - and there was a little man perched way up on top with the wheel in his hands, guiding it. And as I drove along I was struck by the similarity of that machine to the human mind.

Just suppose you are sitting at the controls of such a vast source of energy. Are you going to sit back and fold your arms and let it run itself into a ditch? Or are you going to keep both hands firmly on the wheel and control and direct this power to a specific, worthwhile purpose? It's up to you. You're in the driver's seat.

You see, the very law that gives us success is a two-edged sword. We must control our thinking. The same rule that can lead a man to a life of success, wealth, happiness, and all the things he's ever dreamed of for himself and his family

That very same law can lead him into the gutter. It's all in how he uses it: for good ... or for bad.

This is The Strangest Secret in the world.

Now why do I say it's strange, and why do I call it a secret? Actually, it isn't a secret at all.

It was first promulgated by some of the earliest wise men, and it appears again and again throughout the Bible. But very few people have learned it, understand it. That's why it's strange, and why for some equally strange reason it virtually remains a secret.

I believe that you could go out and walk down the main street of your town and ask one man after another, what the secret of success is and you probably wouldn't run into one man in a month who could tell you.

Now this information is enormously valuable to us if we really understand it and apply it. It's valuable to us not only for our own lives, but the lives of those around us, our family, employees, associates, and friends.

Life should be an exciting adventure. It should never be a bore.

A man should work fully, be alive. He should be glad to get out of bed in the morning. He should be doing a job that he likes to do because he does it well.

One time I heard Grove Patterson make a speech, the editor-in-chief of the Toledo Daily Blade. And as he concluded his speech he said something I've never forgotten. He said something like this, "My years in the newspaper business have convinced me of several things. Among them, that people are basically good, and that we came from someplace and we're going someplace. So we should make our time here an exciting adventure. The architect of the universe didn't build a stairway leading nowhere."

I've explained the Strangest Secret in the World, and how it works. Now I'd like to explain how you can prove to yourself the enormous returns possible in your own life by putting the secret to a practical test.

I want you to make a test that will last 30 days. Not it isn't going to be easy, but if you will give it a good try, it will completely change your life for the better.

Back in the 17th Century, Sir Isaac Newton, the English mathematician and natural philosopher gave us the natural laws of physics, which apply as much to human beings as they do to the movement of bodies in the universe. And one of these laws is: "For every action, there is an equal and opposite reaction".

Simply stated as it applies to you and me, it means we can achieve nothing without paying the price. The results of your 30 day experiment will be in direct proportion to the effort you put forth.

To be a doctor, you must pay the price of long years of difficult study. To be successful in selling, and remember each of us succeeds to the extent of his ability to sell, selling our families on our ideas, selling education in schools, selling our children on the advantages of living a good and honest life, selling our associates and employees on the importance of being exceptional people, to of course, the profession of selling itself.

But to be successful in selling our way of the good life, we must be willing to pay the price. Now what is that price? Well it's many things.

First, it's understanding, emotionally as well as intellectually, that we literally become what we think about, that we must control our thoughts if we're to control our lives. It's understanding fully that, "As ye sow, so shall ye reap."

Secondly, it is cutting away all fetters from the mind and permitting it to soar as it was divinely designed to do. It's the realization that your limitations are self-imposed, and the opportunities for you today are enormous beyond belief. It's rising above narrow-minded pettiness and prejudice.

Thirdly, to use all your courage to force yourself to think positively on your own problem; to set a definite and clearly defined goal for yourself, to let your marvelous mind think about your goal from all possible angles; to let your imagination speculate freely upon many different possible solutions; to refuse to believe there are any circumstances sufficiently strong to defeat you in the accomplishment of your purpose.

To act promptly and decisively when your course is clear and to keep constantly aware of the fact that you are at this moment standing in the middle of your own "**Acres of Diamonds**" as Russell Conwell use to point out.

Fourth, save at least ten percent of what you earn.

It's also remembering that no matter what your present job, it has enormous possibilities, if you are willing to pay the price.

Now let's just go over the important points in the price each of us must pay to achieve the wonderful life that can be ours. It is of course worth any price.

1. You will become what you think about.

2. Remember the word imagination, let your mind soar.

3. Courage, concentrate on your goal every day.

4. Save ten percent of what you earn.

And, Action - Ideas are worthless unless we act on them.

Now I'll try to outline the 30 day test I want you to make. Now keep in mind that you have nothing to lose by making this test, and everything you could possibly want to gain.

There are two things that may be said of everyone:
Each of us wants something, and each of us is afraid of something.

I want you to write on a card what it is you want more than anything else.

It may be more money. Perhaps you'd like to double your income or make a specific amount of money. It may be a beautiful home. It may be success at your job. It may be a particular position in life. It could be a more harmonious family. Each of us wants something.

Write down on your card specifically what it is that you want. Make sure it's a single goal and clearly defined. You needn't show it to anyone, but carry it with you so that you can look at it several times a day.

Think about it in a cheerful, relaxed, positive way each morning when you get up, and immediately you have something to work for - something to get out of bed for, something to live for.

Look at it every chance you get during the day and just before going to bed at night. As you look at it, remember that you must become what you think about, and since you're thinking about your goal, you realize that soon it will be yours. In fact, it's yours really the moment you write it down and begin to think about it.

Look at the abundance all around you as you go about your daily business. You have as much right to this abundance as any other living creature. It's yours for the asking.

Now we come to the difficult part. Difficult because it means the formation of what is probably a brand new habit and new habits are not easily formed. Once formed however, it will follow you for the rest of your life.

Second, stop thinking about what it is you fear.
Each time a fearful or negative thought comes into your consciousness, replace it with a mental picture of your positive and worthwhile goal. There will come times when you'll feel like giving up. It's easier for a human being to think negatively than positively. That's why only five percent are successful!

You must begin now to place yourself in that group. For 30 days you must take control of your mind. It will think only about what you permit it to think. Each day for this 30 day test, do more than you have to do.

In addition to maintaining a cheerful positive outlook, give of yourself more than you've ever done before. Do this knowing that your returns in life must be in direct proportion to what you give.

The moment you decide on a goal to work toward, you're immediately a successful person. You are then in that rare and successful category of people who know where they are going. Out of every 100 people, you belong to the top five.

Don't concern yourself too much with how you're going to achieve your goal. Leave that completely to a power greater than yourself. All you have to do is know where you're going. The answers will come to you of their own accord.

Remember these words from the Sermon On The Mount and remember them well. Keep them constantly before you this month of your test.

"Ask, And It Shall Be Given You"
"Seek, And Ye Shall Find"
"Knock, And It Shall Be Opened Unto You"
"For Every One That Asketh, Receiveth"
"And He That Seeketh, Findeth"
"And To Him That Knocketh, It Shall Be Open"

It's as marvelous and as simple as that. In fact it is so simple, that in our seemingly complicated world, it's difficult for an adult to understand that all he needs is a purpose ... and faith.

For 30 days do your best. If you're a salesman, go at it as you've never done before, not in hectic fashion, but with the calm, cheerful assurance that time well spent will give you the abundance in return you deserve and want.

If you are a homemaker, devote your 30 day test to complete giving of yourself without thinking about receiving anything in return, and you will be amazed at the difference it makes in your life.

No matter what your job do it as you have never done before for 30 days, and if you've kept your goal before you every day you'll wonder and marvel at this new life you've found.

Dorothea Brande, outstanding editor and writer, discovered it for herself and tells about it in her fine book "Wake up and Live". Her entire philosophy is reduced to the words: **"Act as though it were impossible to fail."** She made her own test, with sincerity and faith, and her entire life was changed to one of overwhelming success.

Now, you make *your* test for 30 full days. Don't start your test until you have made up your mind to stick with it. You see by being persistent, you are demonstrating faith. Persistence is simply another word for faith. If you did not have faith, you would never persist.

If you should fail during your first 30 days, by that I mean suddenly find yourself overwhelmed by negative thoughts – you've got to start over again from that point and go 30 more days.

Gradually, your new habit will form, until you find yourself one of that wonderful minority to whom virtually nothing is impossible.

Don't forget the card. It is vitally important as you begin this new way of living.

On one side of the card, write your goal, whatever it may be. On the other side, write the words we've quoted from the Sermon on the Mount.

"Ask, And It Shall Be Given You"
"Seek, And Ye Shall Find"
"Knock, And It Shall Be Opened Unto You"...

In your spare time during your test period read books that will help you. Inspirational books like The Bible, Dorothea Brand's "Wake up and Live" "The Magic of Believing" by Claude Bristol, "Think and Grow Rich" by Napoleon Hill, and **other books** that instruct and inspire.

Nothing great was ever accomplished without inspiration. See that during these crucial first 30 days your own inspiration is kept to a peak.

Above all ... don't worry! Worry brings fear, and fear is crippling. The only thing that can cause you to worry during your test is trying to do it all yourself. Know that all you have to do is hold your goal before you; everything else will take care of itself.

Remember also to keep calm and cheerful, calm and cheerful. Don't let petty things annoy and get you off course.

Now since making this test is difficult, some may say, "Well, Why should I bother?"

Well look at the alternative. No one wants to be a failure. No one really wants to be a mediocre individual. No one wants a life constantly filled with worry, fear and frustration.

Therefore remember that you must reap that which you sow. If you sow negative thoughts, your life will be filled with negative things. If you sow positive thoughts, your life will be cheerful, successful, and positive.

Now gradually you'll have a tendency to forget what you've heard on this record. Play it often. Keep reminding yourself of what you must do to form this new habit. Gather your whole family about and listen to what's been said here at regular intervals.

You know, most men will tell you that they want to make money, without understanding the law. The only people who make money work in the mint. The rest of us must **earn** money.

This is what causes those who keep looking for something for nothing, or a free ride, to fail in life. The only way to earn money is by providing people with services or products which are needed and useful. We exchange our product or service for the other man's money.

Therefore the law is that our financial return will be in direct proportion to our service.

Success is not the result of making money. Making money is the result of success - and success is in direct proportion to our service.

Most people have this law backwards. They believe that you're successful if you earn a lot of money. The truth is that you can only earn money after you're successful.

It's like the story of the man who sat in front of the stove and says to it: "Give me heat and then I'll add the wood." How many men and women do you know, or do you suppose there are today, who take the same attitude toward life? There are millions.

We've got to put the fuel in before we can expect heat. Likewise, we've got to be of service first before we can expect money.

Don't concern yourself with the money. Be of service ... build ... work ...dream ... create! Do this and you'll find there is no limit to the prosperity and abundance that will come to you.

Prosperity is founded upon a law of mutual exchange. Any person who contributes to prosperity must prosper in turn himself.

Sometimes the return will not come from those you serve, but it must come to you from someplace, for that is the law. For every action, there is an equal and opposite reaction.

As you go daily through your 30 day test period, remember that your success will always be measured by the quality and quantity of service you render, and money is a yardstick for measuring this service. No man can get rich himself, unless he enriches others. There are no exceptions to a law.

You can drive down any street in America and from your car estimate the service that's being rendered by the people living on that street.

Have you ever thought of this yardstick before? It's interesting. Some, like ministers, and priests and other devoted people measure their returns in the realm of the spiritual, but again their returns are equal to their service.

Once this law is fully understood, any thinking person can tell his own fortune. If he wants more, he must be of more service to those from whom he receives his return. If he wants less, he has only to reduce this service. This is the price you must pay for what you want.

If you believe you can enrich yourself by deluding others, you can end only by deluding yourself. Just as surely as you breathe, you'll get back what you put out.

Don't ever make the mistake of thinking you can avert this. It's impossible: The prisons and the streets where the lonely walk are filled with people who tried to make new laws just for themselves. We may avoid the laws of man, but there are greater laws that cannot be broken.

An outstanding medical doctor recently pointed out six steps that will help you realize success.

1. Set yourself a definite goal.

2. Quit running yourself down.

3. Stop thinking of all the reasons why you cannot be successful and instead think of all the reasons why you can.

4. Trace your attitudes back through your childhood and try to discover where you first got the idea you couldn't be a success if that is the way you've been thinking.

5. Change the image you have of yourself by writing out a description of the person you would like to be.

6. Act the part of the successful person you have decided to become.

The doctor that wrote those words is a noted west coast psychiatrist, David Harold Fink M.D.

Do what all the experts since the dawn of recorded history have told you you must do: pay the price by becoming the person you want to become. It's not nearly as difficult as living unsuccessfully.

Make your 30 day test, then repeat it ... then repeat it again. Each time it will become more a part of you until you'll wonder how you could have ever have lived any other way. Live this new way and the floodgates of abundance will open and pour over you more riches than you may have dreamed existed.

Money? Yes, lots of it.

But what's more important, you'll have peace ... you'll be in that wonderful minority who lead calm, cheerful, successful lives.

Start today. You have nothing to lose - but you have a life to win.

                          Written in 1956 by Earl Nightingale

About The Author

Jean Kuhn lives in Naperville, Illinois, with her husband Bruce. Jean and Bruce have three adult children, Dennis, Jaclyn, and Matthew. Jean knows fully what it takes to own your own business. She has been self-employed since 1985 when she left the corporate world to be a stay-at-home-*working*-mom. In 1987 Jean found a great, fun, work-from-home sales position with the direct sales multi-level marketing company, House of Lloyd. Jean took the job on a promised trip to Hawaii. If she could hire a team, and her team could hit $40,000 in sales, the trip was hers. Six months, later Jean had earned not one, but TWO free trips to Hawaii. She was hooked on multi-level marketing, and went on to work with two other companies during her career.

1998 brought a new challenge for Jean when she opened and managed a dance studio for children ages 3-18 years old. Jean was neither a dancer, nor a dance teacher, but her passion for believing she can do whatever she sets her mind to, was key to her success. She hired great teachers and even donned a pair of tap shoes when necessary to get a three year old into class. After overcoming extraordinary challenges of this business, Jean sold her studio in 2004.

In 2002 Jean bought a failing Rocky Mountain Chocolate Factory Franchise and quickly turned it around into a cash generating machine. In 2006 Jean bought her second failing franchise location, and again, immediately turned that location around.

Jean started helping fellow franchisee grow their businesses in 2006, but she has been helping small business owners grow their own businesses since 1987. In 2006 Jean founded an annual franchisee conference where she and her fellow franchisees share ideas on marketing strategies, integrated advertising, product ideas, and everything it takes to grow a successful franchise.

In 2009, Jean trained with best-selling author, Bob Burg to become one of his elite Certified Go-Giver Coaches. Jean is passionate about sharing The 5 Laws of Stratospheric Success her clients.

Jean now speaks to franchisees and small business owners all over the country about marketing their businesses to grow their profits.

This workbook is just one of the tools Jean uses in her coaching business because Jean knows you can change your life when you can change your thoughts.

Bonus Offers

Bonus #1

Attention Franchisees!!! Get a complimentary copy of Jean's ebook:

5 Strategies to Higher Profits That Your Franchise Marketing Fee Does Not Cover

Go to www.jeankuhn.com for the free ebook.

Bonus #2

As franchise owners we were given a "business plan" when we purchased our franchises, but that doesn't mean everything will go smoothly all the time. We have the exact same problems as any small business owners. Here are just a couple of the areas where I can assist you.

1. Are you making as much money as you would like?

2. Do you find yourself frustrated in your franchise business almost daily?

3. Do your employees stay awake at night thinking of ways to aggravate you?

If you answered yes to any of these questions, I would like to offer you a complimentary 30 minute strategy session to help you have the business of your dreams. https://jeankuhn.acuityscheduling.com/

Made in United States
Orlando, FL
01 August 2023